WHAT TOMMY TOOK TO WAR 1914–1918

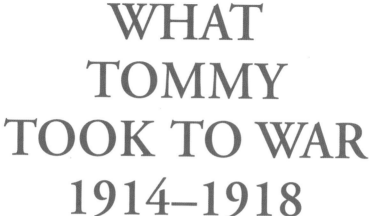

Peter Doyle
and Chris Foster

SHIRE PUBLICATIONS

Published in Great Britain in 2014 by Shire Publications Ltd, PO Box 883, Oxford, OX1 9PL, UK.

PO Box 3985, New York, NY 10185-3985, USA.

E-mail: shire@shirebooks.co.uk   www.shirebooks.co.uk

A CIP catalogue record for this book is available from the British Library.

Shire General no. 7.   ISBN-13: 978 0 74781 403 0

Peter Doyle and Chris Foster have asserted their rights under the Copyright, Designs and Patents Act, 1988, to be identified as the authors of this book.

Designed by Tony Truscott Designs, Sussex, UK.
Typeset in Garamond, Perpetua and Gill Sans.
Printed in China through Worldprint Ltd.

14 15 16 17 18   10 9 8 7 6 5 4 3 2 1

DEDICATION
For Richard Holmes.

ACKNOWLEDGEMENTS
We are grateful to all those who have helped us shape this book. We thank Ted Peacock and Laurie Milner for access to their impressive collections; Taff Gillingham and Foz of Khaki Devil Ltd for their historical interpretation; and Libby Simpson for advice and ideas. Many other people have helped shape our ideas; we are grateful to them all. Michael Hargraves kindly supplied the image of Herbert Longthorne, and Peter Clarke contributed the story of the Mancktelow brothers. We thank those closest to us for their unwavering support:
Julie, James and Sari.

CONTENTS

The Great War and
Tommy Atkins 4–16

What Tommy took
to war 17

Good-luck Charm 18

Sweetheart Jewellery 20

Training Manuals 22

Scoring Booklet 24

Salisbury Plain Cap Badge 26

Semaphore Cards 28

Sports Medals 30

Paybook 32

Cap 34

Glengarry 36

Wolseley-pattern helmet 38

Cap Badge 40

Formation Sign 42

Identity Discs 44

Boots 46

Holdall 48

Spoon 50

Clasp Knife 52

Mess Tins 54

Shaving Kit 56

Cleaning Kit 58

Officers' Kit 60

Webley Mark VI 62

Trench Whistle 64

Smoking 66

Wristwatch 68

Letters 70

Phrase Book 72

Steel Helmet 74

SMLE Rifle 76

1907-pattern Bayonet 78

Entrenching Tool 80

Barbed-wire Cutters 82

Trench Maps 84

SBR (Gas Mask) 86

Mills Bomb 88

Grenade Badges 90

Trench Knives 92

Rum Jar 94

Diaries 96

Testament 98

Leave Pass 100

Trench Art 102

Silk Postcards 104

Field Dressing 106

Stretcher-bearer
Armband 108

Casualty Letter 110

Wounded Stripes 112

Medals 114

Poppy 116

Index 118

THE GREAT WAR AND TOMMY ATKINS

The British Soldier of the First World War – almost universally referred to as 'Tommy Atkins' by the public – fought campaigns across three continents. When the war commenced he was very much a regular soldier: highly trained, well equipped, and capable of facing even a most determined enemy. Arriving in France in August 1914, the British Expeditionary Force was composed of regulars; but by the end of the year, dwindling in numbers, they were bolstered by territorials – part-time soldiers who had originally signed up only for home defence. Most volunteered for overseas service at the outbreak of war, and were formed into 'First Line' territorial battalions to fight in France. With Lord Kitchener all too aware that the war would be a long one, his direct call for volunteers in 100,000 tranches was instrumental in supplying the manpower of Britain's armies from late 1915 onwards. It was the Kitchener volunteer who would fight on the Somme in 1916, but arguably, it was conscription that created the army that won the war in 1918, a function of the Military Service Act of 1916. In all cases, men came from all walks of life and from all backgrounds.

Starting from an initial number of just six regular infantry divisions (1st–6th) in 1914, the War Office assembled a further six regular divisions, thirty New Army divisions, twenty-nine Territorial divisions, a Yeomanry division, three Home Service divisions, and one compiled from Royal Naval Reservists – the Royal Naval Division. Of this total of seventy-six available, sixty-five would see action overseas. In addition to the infantry, there were three cavalry divisions, comprising around nine thousand men. Each infantry division was made up of almost twenty thousand men, of whom the greatest number, comprising in the early part of the war some twelve thousand men divided between three infantry brigades (in turn composed of three infantry battalions each), were infantry proper. The remainder was composed of the fighting arms such as the Artillery and Engineers (making up some five thousand men), and the Services, such as the Army Service Corps – required to supply the needs of the division in the field – and

Pte R W S Tylee
m.t. 286

IS SERVING HIS

KING   COUNTRY

AND
EMPIRE

COPYRIGHT

'Serving his King, Country and Empire': a card displayed in the window of a family house. Private Tylee, a motor transport driver, survived the war.

the Royal Army Medical Corps – expected to support and aid the sick and wounded. And there were many other services, all vital to the British war effort.

For the most part, the Western Front – the western theatre of operations for Imperial Germany – demanded most attention and consumed men and materiel in ever increasing numbers. In late 1914 the Western Front became a continuous line of trenches from Switzerland to the North Sea, 475 miles across varied terrain; and by the end of the war British and Empire troops occupied some 120 miles of the front, in the historically strategic zone that straddled the Franco-Belgian border, extending southwards deep into Picardy. Engaged from August 1914 at the Battle of Mons, the British Expeditionary Force was to grow in size and stature to become the backbone of the Allied effort in the closing months of 1918 in the campaigns that defeated Imperial Germany – with 5,399,563 Empire troops employed on the Western Front alone, the vast majority from the United Kingdom.

Away from the Western Front, the British soldier was engaged at Gallipoli, in a costly and unsuccessful attempt to defeat the Ottoman Empire in European Turkey. The campaign lasted from April 1915 to January 1916 and claimed the second biggest total of British casualties at 112,040; it ended

Opposite right: A soldier of the Western Front: Private Herbert Longthorne pictured in 1918. Private Longthorne served in the 7th (Rifle) Battalion, West Yorkshire Regiment, joining the army on 2 November 1917 at the age of eighteen. He was wounded exactly one year later, to the day – just nine days before the Armistice. He carries 1914-pattern leather equipment and the SMLE rifle.

in ignominious withdrawal. The Ottomans were engaged elsewhere across the Middle East: in Mesopotamia (modern Iraq), an initially successful British advance past Basra led to a crushing surrender to the Turks at Kut-al-Amara in 1916, which would not be reversed until 1918; in Palestine and the Arabian peninsula, the scene of the exploits of T. E. Lawrence ('Lawrence of Arabia'), the British would be more successful, and the Ottomans were to sue for peace in late October 1918 after Edmund Allenby had taken Jerusalem.

At Salonika in mainland Greece, the Mediterranean Expeditionary Force (MEF) faced the Bulgarians and their German allies from 1916. Here, more men were lost to disease than as battle casualties. In 1918 the MEF participated in a co-ordinated offensive over difficult terrain, forcing the capitulation of Bulgaria in September 1918 – the first of the Central Powers to surrender. There were numerous other theatres – in South West Africa, for example, and to bolster the hard-pressed Italians in the valley of the Isonzo in Slovenia. Further afield, in the opening days of the war, there was Tsingtao, in China, and at its close Archangel, in northern Russia. The British soldier went wherever he was needed.

The khaki uniform worn by the British soldier was first introduced in 1902, a development of the cotton

Opposite left:
A soldier of the Queen's (Royal West Kent Regiment) in c. 1916. He wears the typical serge service dress and stiff cap.

Opposite right:
A soldier of the Gordon Highlanders, with kilt, sporran and glengarry, c. 1915. He wears Highland shoes and spats – impractical in the front line.

Service Dress of khaki used in the Boer War of 1899–1902. This serge uniform was designed to suit all purposes; when the army put its ceremonial red coats into storage at the outbreak of the war, it would be some time before they were seen again. The Service Dress jacket was loose-fitting, with five brass buttons bearing the royal arms, a turned-down collar, and patches at the shoulder to bear the extra wear from the position of the rifle butt in action. It had a pair of box-pleated patch pockets at the upper chest, and a pair of deep pockets let into the tunic skirt. Shoulder straps bore regimental insignia in the form of brass shoulder titles. Accompanying the jacket was a pair of trousers finished in wool serge with a narrow leg, and worn with puttees, while mounted soldiers wore breeches tightly laced over the calves.

Not all soldiers wore woollen Service Dress, however; a cotton version, known as Khaki Drill, was worn in places with a hot climate such as Mesopotamia or Gallipoli, topped off with a Wolseley-pattern cork helmet for sun protection.

Puttees were worn throughout the war, providing a covering for the lower leg that gave support and protection and prevented grit and dirt from entering the boot tops. Learning how to tie the puttee soon became a mark of the experienced soldier. Consisting of long woollen serge strips provided with cotton tapes, puttees were wound around the leg from the ankle to the knee by the average infantryman. Mounted soldiers (including cavalrymen, artillerymen and Army Service Corps men) were distinguished by their practice of winding the puttee from the knee to the ankle.

Highland Scots regiments were usually kilted, with a bewildering array of regimental patterns of dress, based on regulation patterns of tartan. The kilt was worn in full dress with a sporran, Highland shoes, hose tops and spats – but in the front line the Scots soldier more often than not wore boots, socks and puttees (long or short patterns according to battalion preference), with the colourful kilt covered with an apron.

Each infantryman was equipped with a rifle and an equipment set designed to carry the extra clothing and other small items needed to support him in the field. The full 1908-pattern webbing equipment consisted of belt, cross-straps, cartridge carriers (designed to carry 150 rounds in ten pouches, each holding three five-round chargers), water bottle, bayonet frog, and entrenching tool in its

Opposite:
A soldier wearing Khaki Drill and a Wolseley-pattern helmet, Egypt, c. 1917.

An infantryman tying puttees.

webbing head carrier; the helve for the entrenching tool was strapped to the scabbard of the bayonet. In addition, there was a small haversack, and a large pack, with cross-straps to keep it in place, balancing the weight of the cartridge carriers in front; previous equipment sets had the disadvantage of pulling up the belt and creating imbalance. The average infantryman's uniform and equipment added up to around 60 pounds, a weight that is typical for front-line soldiers even today.

Not all British soldiers were equipped with 1908 webbing, however. With the huge influx of men into the armed forces at the beginning of the Great War, the Mills Equipment Company was seriously overstretched, and a stopgap was needed. The 1914 pattern that followed was based on the format of the webbing but was made from leather, which was quicker to manufacture, and easier to source from overseas manufacturers. This pattern was typical of men from the Kitchener's Army battalions. Other soldiers, not serving in the infantry, commonly wore leather equipment first designed in 1903. This is distinguished by its impressive-looking ammunition bandolier that was worn across the chest by men of the Field Artillery or Army Service Corps.

Well-equipped, appropriately clothed, and carrying the most effective bolt-action rifle of the time, the British soldier fought on six fronts. Yet, while the objects illustrated in this

Far left:
An infantryman
of the Middlesex
Regiment in
'marching order',
fully equipped
with 1908-pattern
webbing equipment
and SMLE rifle.

Left:
An infantryman
of the Middlesex
Regiment
showing the rear
arrangement of
equipment in the
1908 webbing set.

book make some connection between the men and their war, it is difficult to express the scale of loss suffered by the combatants of the First World War. While most men did return, it was common for families to experience tragedy. The story of Alfred and Isabella Mancktelow of Poplar, London, is by no means unusual. On 21 November 1914 their eldest son, Herbert, just eighteen, was killed at the Battle of Ypres while serving as a regular soldier with the 1st Battalion Duke of Cornwall's Light Infantry. His body was never recovered, and his name is now a line on the Menin Gate, which today guards the road to the Old Front Line, and where, every night, the Last Post is sounded in his memory and that of 54,389 others. No doubt hoping that the war would be over before it overshadowed their lives again, Alfred and Isabella had to face the fact that another son came of military age just as the war seemed certain to draw to a close. Called to the colours and serving as a rifleman in the King's Royal Rifle Corps, Horace Mancktelow's life was also claimed by the brutality of the Ypres Salient. He lies in the Messines Ridge British Cemetery, killed in action on 28 September 1918. Reunited in death, the names of the Mancktelow brothers killed at the commencement and closure of one of the most terrible wars in history are listed on their local memorial.

Far left: Right-hand cartridge carriers of the 1908 webbing set.

Below far left: Water bottle and cradle of the 1908 webbing set.

A soldier of the Army Service Corps with 1903-pattern bandolier, commonly issued to mounted soldiers.

The war memorial at Poplar, London, bearing the names of Herbert and Horace Mancktelow.

WHAT TOMMY TOOK TO WAR

GOOD-LUCK CHARM

The vast majority of British soldiers were newly recruited to the colours. The British army of 1914 stood at just 400,000; by the end of the war it had expanded tenfold to some four million, men derived from all walks of life, both volunteers and conscripts. It is inevitable that within this rich diversity of men there would be those who were naturally superstitious. And in waving goodbye to their men, relatives and sweethearts also put their trust in luck. In the early stages of the war there were several commercially available charms to back up their beliefs, including 'Fums-up', a silver charm with rotating arms and erect thumbs. With 'thumbs up' an ancient hand symbol indicating simply 'I'm OK', the charm was finished off with a wooden head, thereby, it was hoped, providing the means to ensure well-being. The idea of 'touching wood' as an act to avert the inevitability of fate was an ancient superstition, bound up, perhaps, with appeasing the 'wood spirits'. Whatever its purpose, many resorted to 'touching wood' after tempting fate. For this reason, another charm – 'Tommy Touchwud' – was equipped with a large bulbous wooden head, which could be touched in the pocket, and may have given some reassurance. Aimed squarely at the soldiers' market, Mr Touchwud was fitted with Tommy's khaki cap, a direct alignment with military men. Whether such charms were actually prized by the market they were intended for is another matter, and this one stayed resolutely in its box. Perhaps homespun versions were more popular and meaningful: tiny toys from soldiers' children, lucky pennies, shrapnel and spent bullets from near misses. Naturally, crucifixes were also carried by some men, typically worn with identity discs around the neck to give both comfort and protection.

SWEETHEART JEWELLERY

In Britain and abroad, soldiers found opportunity to pledge their love to wives, sweethearts and family through the purchase – or manufacture – of small pieces of unpretentious jewellery. These were worn by the recipient in memory of a loved one 'on active service'. At home, the use of uniform buttons was popular. The standard uniform button worn by most soldiers bore the royal arms, and pin brooches made from two or more buttons were produced for the mass market of British soldiery. More elaborate versions included the addition of silver mounts to buttons, particularly typical of the elite rifle regiments, who wore distinctive black, bugle-horn buttons. In other cases, mass-produced mother-of-pearl brooches with silver fittings and silver and enamel representations of regimental badges were made for the jewellers' market; more up-market versions were made from tortoiseshell and silver. Also distinctive – but perhaps a little more obscure – were small silver and glass pin brooches that contained the regimental colours. This one bears a green-white-green regimental flash of the Worcestershire Regiment, redolent of the uniform facings worn with red coats by this ancient regiment. Later in the war, other versions of the same brooch were made to contain ribbons of hard-won gallantry medals – the distinctive red-blue-red of the Distinguished Conduct Medal or the white-purple-white of the Military Cross. 'Sweethearts' like these were extremely popular throughout the war, while others were made by soldier artisans, constructed as 'trench art' from scraps of metal, buttons, badges and the like – actual reminders of the activity, and of the men, in the front line.

C.D.S. 313. OFFICIAL COPY.

[Crown Copyr...

FIELD ALM...
1917.

40
W.O.
3472

(Official)
S.S. 182. FOR OFFICIAL USE ONLY.

INSTRUCTIONS ON BOMBING.

[Crown Copyright Reserved.]

PART I.

...MAN BOMBS.

...AL STAFF.

[Crown Copyright Reserved.

BAYONET FIGHTING.

INSTRUCTION WITH SERVICE RIFLE AND BAYONET.

1915.

WHAT EVERY SOLDIER OUGHT TO KNOW

COMPILED FROM
THE OFFICIAL MANUALS

Price Twopence

OXFORD UNIVERSITY PRESS
HUMPHREY MILFORD
1915

TRAINING MANUALS

The average recruit was supposed to undergo a prescribed training period of six months. The official manuals set out this syllabus in 1914; there would be fitness training, fieldcraft, musketry and bayonet fighting. Bringing a civilian to a state of readiness where he was fit enough to tackle any threat thrown at him, was able to live out in all weathers, and was proficient in handling his weapons was no mean task. The main manual for training was *Infantry Training 1914*; issued six days after war was declared, it was intended as a guide for officers engaged in the training of new recruits. The training period was divided into fortnights of activity: soldiers spent most of their time in physical training, before learning the squad drill and musketry that would equip them to fight under orders – while facing their enemies. Though six months was the ideal, all too often this was reduced as the needs for men at the front increased, and the original training period was soon reduced to three months. After the initial training, and even after being sent to the front, the soldier could expect to receive further instruction, and the War Office issued a constant stream of documents that served up the knowledge gathered from the experience of the trenches. Grenade fighting, improvements to bayonet training, gas drill, field defences – all came under review. And for the average soldier, intent on keeping his head down and getting back to Blighty, 'What Every Soldier Ought to Know' was an essential reference.

SCORING BOOK

FOR THE

GENERAL MUSKETRY COURSE

AND

COURSE FOR JAPANESE RIFLE
AND CARBINE

WITH HINTS ON HOW TO SHOOT.

No. .... Rank .... Name ....

Coy. .... Regt.

THIS BOOK ALWAYS TO BE TAKEN
ON THE RANGE.

Published by JOHN McQUEEN & SON, Target Manufacturers,
GALASHIELS, Scotland.

Price—2d each.   Quantity Prices on Application.

SCORING BOOKLET

The War Office manual *Musketry Regulations Part 1, 1909 (Reprinted with Amendments, 1914)* defined the basis for rifle training with the soldier's rifle, the Short Magazine Lee Enfield or SMLE: 'to render the individual soldier proficient in the use of small arms, to make him acquainted with the capabilities of the weapon with which he is armed, and to give him confidence in its power and accuracy.' As well as hearing lectures on the theory of rifle firing, the recruit was taken through his paces to learn the fundamentals before progressing to actually firing his weapon. Practice rounds, with wooden 'bullets', were issued for this purpose. This was all well and good, but maintaining supply of the standard SMLE to the vast influx of new soldiers was a serious problem. With the supply of rifles being just enough to meet the mobilisation needs of the army in 1914 – and production taking some time to attain sustainable levels – many new soldiers were issued with older or obsolete rifles, or even ones that had been bought in from overseas, from Canada, India, the United States or even Japan. The Japanese supplied 130,000 Arisaka rifles for training – but only for training, because the bullet calibre of the Japanese rifle was not consistent with the .303 SMLE (and therefore specially produced rounds were required for it). In all cases, firing practice on the ranges ensured that all recruits received at least a basic grounding in musketry skills, involving the practice of grouping shots, or selective shooting at specific targets. Special target books were produced for soldiers to record their progress to becoming a rifleman; this one, for the Arisaka, was the property of Private James Turnbull of the King's Own Scottish Borderers, who would see action in Egypt in 1917 – and survive the war.

SALISBURY PLAIN
CAP BADGE

Salisbury Plain, a tract of well-drained chalk downland 20 miles long and 16 miles wide in southern England, has been the location of military activity for centuries, but from the late nineteenth century the Plain became famous as the site of military training activities and, with the formation of the Territorial Force in 1908, the location of many encampments for soldiers in training. The War Department bought up large tracts of the land and set about constructing barracks that would be suitable for the accommodation of large numbers of soldiers. But these very soon became swamped with the influx of Kitchener's volunteers, and the Plain was transformed into a sea of canvas as tented encampments sprang up across the landscape. Though many of these camps were replaced by wooden huts in 1915, conditions were basic. Arriving in 1914 were Private Humphrey Mason and his father, Corporal Benjamin Mason, who enlisted together in the 6th Battalion Oxfordshire and Buckinghamshire Light Infantry – a Kitchener's Army battalion that formed part of the 'second hundred thousand', the second tranche of soldiers who answered Lord Kitchener's call. Engaged in six months' training, the battalion was housed in wooden huts on the plain. Chipping off a piece of the chalk foundation of his hut, Humphrey Mason carved an exact copy of his regimental cap badge. Though he expected it to be 'smashed in the post', Mason's carving nevertheless survived in a tobacco tin as a relic of one soldier's period in training.

Y

Called YORKER.

Brown's "VICK" SEMAPHORE CARDS

Self-Instruction

Self-Examination

9d. net.

Thus to form the letter **Q** the right arm is at position **B** and the left at **E**.

Signs should be made facing the receiver, and accuracy of angles is most essential.

All numbers to be spelt out as words.

General Rules to be observed by a person

SEMAPHORE CARDS

According to the 1916 manual *Signalling*, 'The various ranks and services of an army in the field may be compared to parts of the human body. Thus the general in supreme command … is its brain; the aircraft, cavalry and scouts constitute its eyes and ears; while the signallers, messengers … who carry his orders to every unit of his force, represent its nervous system.' Signalling was, and is, necessary in warfare, and in the days before reliable wireless communications it was necessary to train soldiers adequately in the application and use of military signalling techniques. In the Great War these techniques included visual signalling (the use of semaphore, heliograph or lights), despatch riders, and telephone. Despatch riders, mounted on motorcycles or even bicycles, were effective in the rear areas – and their place would be taken by designated 'runners' in the front line, when telephones failed. Telephony was the quickest method, but it required the Army Signal Service to lay considerable amounts of wire, which were constantly interrupted in the front line by shelling. In daylight, semaphore was another possibility, particularly in the open conditions of the Middle East. It required just a few trained men who could wield large flags, moving them into set positions and thereby spelling out an alphabet of letters that could be noted down to form the message. The two flags were of differing types: both 3 feet square, one was white with a blue stripe, the other blue. Qualified instructors were denoted by crossed flags on their upper right arms. Knowledge of the semaphore alphabet necessitated learning the flag positions by rote – and commercial suppliers soon stepped in to provide aids.

SPORTS MEDALS

'The object of physical training is the production of a state of health and physical fitness in order that the body may be enabled to withstand the strains of daily life and to perform the work required of it without injury to the system' (*Manual of Physical Training 1914*). The army placed great store in developing the man through physical training. As part of the syllabus of training expected of a recruit, route marches and runs were supplemented with a complex series of gymnastic exercises that were based on the Swedish system developed in the late nineteenth century. Often referred to disparagingly as 'physical jerks', they were meant to give attention to the whole body. While the value of these seemed obscure to some trainees, the opportunity to engage in competitive sports was more readily understood. Boxing, athletics, rugby and football were extremely popular and easy to organise – especially as some recruits were skilled sportsmen in their own right. Kitchener's Army boasted Footballers' and Sportsmen's battalions – in the Middlesex Regiment and Royal Fusiliers respectively – and many other units had their fair share of athletes. For instance, at Loos in September 1915 the London Irish Rifles, famed for their footballing prowess, kicked off the battle with their footballs. Football and other games were deemed essential to the maintenance of morale, and medals and silver fobs were routinely given out to cup-winners, at home and in France. This one, awarded for inter-company football winners in the 24th Division in 1917–18, is typical. The 24th, a division of Kitchener's Army, had been badly mauled at Loos in 1915 but went on to rebuild its reputation in 1916–18. No doubt sports played some part in this.

PAYBOOK

As part of their official record of service, soldiers were issued with a document that served as a logbook of their service, including personal and family details (such as next of kin), regimental number, dates of enlistment, ranks and awards attained, skill at arms, charges, a sick record, and a record of pay issued. Before the war, the soldier was issued with a linen-covered 'Small Book' that was filled with nuggets of information intended to be of value to him. In time of war, and on service overseas, the most important document was the AB64, the 'Soldier's Service and Pay Book', issued to every soldier who was on active service. Stored in the right breast pocket of the uniform jacket, the paybook was to be carried at all times and had to be produced on request for examination by officers or regimental and military police. The AB64 was therefore a valuable document, proof of identification both as a battlefield casualty, and when receiving pay. The paybook also recorded issues of uniform, inoculations, 'crimes' and pay stoppages for acts as trivial as the loss of a cap badge, and evidence of gas training. Tellingly, page thirteen of the AB64 was a will; soldiers moving up the line for the first time were expected to complete this before going into battle. For most, this would include a simple statement leaving all that he possessed to his wife and children.

CAP

In 1914 British soldiers, like all other combatants of the day, went to war in headgear that was quite unsuited to modern warfare. Finding adequate protection for the head would have to wait for a year's experience of war. For the French there would be the kepi; for the Germans, the ornate *pickelhaube*; for Tommy it would be the peaked cap that was adopted in 1905, with stiffened rim and peak, and bearing the traditional cap badge of the British army. The stiffness of this headgear made it awkward. The example illustrated is a rare survivor, shaped by a soldier from the Royal Sussex Regiment who fitted an officer's cap badge. In late 1914, an answer to the impracticality of this headgear was the issue of the winter trench cap. Known universally as the 'gor-blimey', this soon became shapeless with wear, but it was a comfortable cap with flaps that could be fastened under the chin for extra warmth, or stowed on top of the cap – adding to its ungainly appearance. The gor-blimey, never a favourite with sergeant-majors (hence its nickname), was to be replaced by the issue of the 1917-pattern cap. This was capable of being folded and stowed in the soldier's equipment, as it had no stiff components, a stitched peak being the only concession to smartness – a unique feature of late-war 'trench' caps. The 1917-pattern cap had a black oilcloth or cotton khaki lining and was comfortable to wear; Tommy also often personalised it by plaiting the leather strap, while parting the strap components was also popular. A final modification was the issue of a denim version in 1918, again with the same linings.

GLENGARRY

While the vast majority of soldiers wore the Service Dress cap, for the Scots there was a range of bonnets to complement the appearance of the typically kilted Highland soldier. It was uncommon for Scots soldiers to don a peaked cap. Early in the war the commonest bonnet was the glengarry, found in a variety of patterns: plain dark blue with a red tuft or 'tourie' (worn by the Black Watch and Cameron Highlanders); rifle green with a black tourie (Cameronians and Highland Light Infantry); red and white diced border and red tourie (Argyll and Sutherland Highlanders, fitted with their distinctively large white-metal cap badge, as illustrated); and finally red-green-white diced borders with red tourie (Royal Scots, Royal Scots Fusiliers, King's Own Scottish Borderers, Seaforth Highlanders and Gordon Highlanders). There were other regiments who adopted the glengarry too; the Territorial 10th Battalion of the King's Liverpool Regiment, the Liverpool Scottish, wore the red-white-green diced border, while the Kitchener's Army battalions of the Northumberland Fusiliers known as the Tyneside Scottish adopted a plain dark blue glengarry with red tourie and black silk rosette. Impractical in the field, and offering no protection from the elements, the glengarry was replaced in 1915, first by the beret-like Balmoral bonnet, and then by the serge khaki Tam O'Shanter bonnet, a large, circular but otherwise shapeless object that nonetheless distinguished the Scot.

WOLSELEY-PATTERN HELMET

While soldiers on the Western Front wore the standard woollen serge uniform, a cotton uniform known as Khaki Drill or 'KD' was the standard issue for warm climates. It was basically a cotton version of the standard serge Service Dress, but there were some significant differences. Cotton KD was of a lighter khaki colour than the serge Service Dress, its jacket fastened by five buttons that were attached to it by loops to facilitate removal for laundry purposes. Trousers were issued with the jacket, but more often than not shorts were worn with socks and puttees. KDs were usually worn with the Wolseley-pattern cork sun helmet, a 'solar topee', which protected only from the sun – its protection enhanced by the use of additional neck flaps. The helmet illustrated is typical, though is likely to be that of an officer (distinguished by its leather rim; other ranks' helmets had cotton edging). Equipped with a 'puggaree', a long strip of cotton wound as if in a turban, the helmet would be quite often worn with a distinctive battalion flash. Khaki Drill and Wolseley helmets were worn in East Africa, India, Egypt, Gallipoli, Salonika and while on imperial service anywhere in the hotter corners of the British Empire. In many cases, blue-grey shirts alone were worn, in 'shirt sleeve order', and in the hottest climates, as in Mesopotamia, 'spine-pads' were issued, a vain provision to prevent the sun beating down on the spine, a supposed preventative for sunstroke. This particular innovation did nothing but add to the heat exhaustion of the average soldier in the deserts of the Middle East.

CAP BADGE

With the adoption of the Service Dress cap in 1905 the continued role of the cap badge – first introduced in the late nineteenth century (replacing a range of helmet plates) – was assured. The cap badge served in peace and war to distinguish the regiment. Since the Cardwell reforms of the late nineteenth century, regiments had become regional organisations with constituent battalions tied to a home depot, thereby providing a mechanism for local recruitment. Most badges were constructed from brass, others from 'white metal', or a combination of the two ('bimetal'); bronze insignia were generally the mark of an officer. In the trenches, badges were often removed to hinder identification in case of capture. In most cases, regulars, Territorials and Kitchener men wore the same badge – the new battalions adopting the regimental traditions of the old, though Territorial battalions were often denied the battle honours of their regular cousins. While most Kitchener men wore their county badge, a few battalions of 'Pals', raised in the patriotic fervour at the outbreak of war, demanded their own distinctive insignia. With uniforms in short supply, Pals' battalions were often distinguished by a simple device. An enamel 'Birmingham Battalion' badge was issued by the Lord Mayor of Birmingham in lieu of uniform. This was replaced by a special version of the county badge with added scroll – and was worn with special brass titles borne on the shoulder straps of the uniform. These insignia were all the property of one man, an original 'Birmingham Pal', his name now sadly obscure.

FORMATION SIGN

With so many units in the field by 1916–17, an effective system of identifying them as components of a larger formation was needed, to be used widely on the transport, headquarters and, later, the men themselves. Left largely to the whim of the commanders of these units, a series of identifying badges was developed that could be painted on battalion transport and the like. Late in the war, versions were sewn to the upper sleeve of the soldiers' Service Dress. Often colourful, they commonly made reference to the regional origin of the formation, like the thistle of the 9th (Scottish) Division or the red rose of the 55th (West Lancashire) Division. In other cases they used a symbol that indicated the number or origin of the division – such as the bantam cock of the 40th Division, raised as a 'bantam' division of under-height men, or the broken spur of the 74th Division, composed largely of dismounted Yeomanry troops. Some were cryptic, such as the 'ATN' symbol of the 18th (Eastern) Division, or obscure, such as the butterfly of the 19th (Western) Division. That of the 38th (Welsh) Division was more obvious – the traditional red dragon of Wales. The Welsh Division was raised in the early days of the war, composed of Welsh Kitchener's Army men, who had been impelled to join by David Lloyd George's patriotic fervour. The Division was composed of men from the country's regiments and support services, all of whom would sport the dragon on their upper arms. As one contemporary poet put it in the 1918 *Souvenir of the Welsh Division*, 'Borderers, Welsh and Fusiliers, / Guns and Mortars and Engineers, / Machine-gun Wallahs and Pioneers, / We're the Welsh, the 38th.'

IDENTITY DISCS

Identity discs – known as 'cold-meat tickets' to the British soldiery of the Great War – have not always been worn in battle. The first tags were a mid-nineteenth-century German innovation, while the British Army resorted to the use of an identity card in the uniform pocket – hardly durable. Clearly inadequate, this form of identification was replaced in 1907 by a single stamped aluminium disc, which carried the soldier's name, rank, serial number, unit details and his religion. Issued to soldiers on mobilisation, the valuable aluminium was replaced by fibre in August 1914. These discs were much more appropriate than identity cards, but they had their problems; if this single disc was removed from the body, as stipulated in the 1909 *Field Service Regulations*, the chances of identification of the body were much reduced. Therefore, in August 1916, a two-disc system was evolved, the discs themselves carrying the same information as before, in duplicate, but this time stamped on compressed fibre discs: a green octagonal one that, it was intended, would stay with the body, and a red disc that would be taken as part of the accounting procedure. Both were to be worn on a string around the neck, the red disc suspended from the green one. Unfortunately, neither disc would last long in the damp conditions of much of the Western Front. Perhaps because of this, few soldiers had absolute faith in the discs and many commissioned or made their own identity bracelets, to be worn on the wrist. Sergeant Humphrey Mason, transferred from the infantry to the Machine Gun Corps, put his trust in a copper wristlet, worn alongside the issue discs.

BOOTS

During the war, the traditional centre of shoemaking, Northampton, was stretched to capacity in supplying boots, not only for the British army, but also for most of the Allies in the field, employed on all fronts. Even during peacetime, some 245,000 pairs of boots were required annually to supply the British Army, and this had to increase dramatically during the war. The 'regulation' British field boot for most of the war was roughly square-toed, produced in thick hide with the rough side out. The soles of these boots were cleated with metal studs, which covered almost the whole of the sole in the standard infantryman's boot, or simply the toe area for mounted soldiers, who had to use stirrups. Soldiers issued with the boots for field use were instructed to pack the rough leather with dubbin in order to create a more water-resistant material, and this produced the tan colour that is so typical of the field boot. Blackened boots were more common at home. The standard pattern early in the war was the B2 (first introduced in 1913); the later B5 boot (illustrated), identified by its distinctive quarters and copper rivet, was widely introduced in 1915–16. Late in the war, a further boot pattern was introduced, with a distinctive crescent toecap. Among other footwear used by Tommy on the Western Front were the high boots of the mounted artilleryman, and the so-called 'trench waders', made by the North British Rubber Company in Scotland, and centrally held as 'trench stores'.

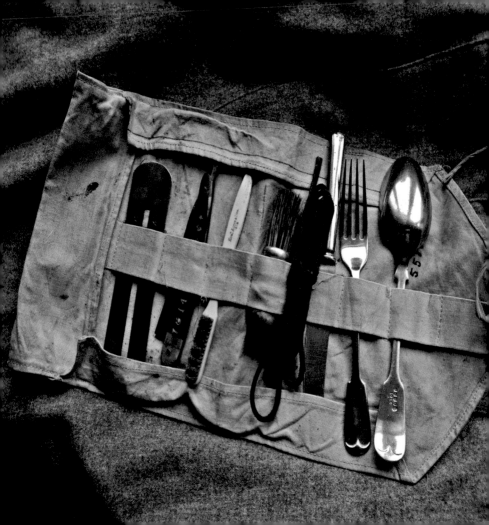

HOLDALL

The holdall was a cloth wrap with loops to hold items of equipment in place, the material used changing through the war from a stiff canvas to a thin cotton cloth roll. The contents and manufacture of the holdall varied throughout the soldier's career, and each man was expected to mark these small items of equipment with his regimental number (or the last four digits) and his regiment or corps, using a punch for metal objects, or ink for cloth. The first issue of what the army called 'necessaries' was made on joining, and this was the soldier's 'free kit'. After this, it was up to the soldier to fill his holdall and keep it up to date, though 'no departure from the articles detailed in the lists' issued by the War Office was permitted. The canvas holdall illustrated contains (from left to right): a button brass, essential to keep metal polish from staining the uniform – these were stamped with the regimental number and battalion; a cut-throat razor marked to the soldier (with his number) and his battalion; a toothbrush, essential as the army put great store in maintaining oral health (without teeth, soldiers would struggle to eat the food issued); a shaving brush, of many different patterns – soldiers had to replace them at their own expense; spare boot laces – leather ones were used; and knife, fork and spoon – there are several different patterns known. In the field, knives were probably discarded. In accordance with regulation, cutlery was also stamped with the soldier's regimental number and battalion. The holdall had a convenient pocket that provided the means of carrying additional small items.

SPOON

Though the first issue of 'necessaries' included the knife, fork and spoon, in the front line it was the spoon that was the most highly prized piece of cutlery. Stamped with at least the last four digits of a soldier's regimental number (a precaution against the universal practice of 'scrounging' or 'winning'), fork and spoon are commonly encountered, but knives less so, suggesting that they were discarded in favour of the 'jack' or clasp knife worn on a string lanyard around the waist. Pictured in one of the most famous photographs of the war, two Vickers machine-gunners carry this most useful of all utensils in the most convenient place of all – tucked into the tops of their puttees. In this way the spoons were always available, without the need to unbuckle equipment. Often, as in this case, the spoon was worn down through use – and even sharpened so as to be transformed into a multi-purpose utensil. This spoon was the property of a soldier in the 6th Battalion, King's Own Scottish Borderers, 7467 Private William Richardson. Well used, Private Richardson's spoon has also been sharpened so it could be used in cutting food. As most meals in the front line were simple rations, such a spoon was all that was needed. The regimental numbers impressed into substantial items such as this serve as more than a simple expression of ownership: recovered with a soldier's remains, they help provide a means of identification. In this case, Private Richardson was not carrying his spoon when he went into action at the Battle of Loos on 25 September 1915. 'Missing presumed dead', his body was never recovered, his spoon left behind as a remembrance of the man.

CLASP KNIFE

The clasp knife was one of the most important pieces of personal kit, used for duties as diverse as trench repair, tin-opening and eating – the daintier knife from the holdall being jettisoned or lost as the war dragged on. The army clasp knife of the First World War was a substantial piece of kit, measuring some 5 inches long, with a heavy 3½-inch-long blade, and black, chequered horn grips (though other patterns are known, from brown horn to plain slab-steel sides). The majority of knives were fitted with a marline spike, a steel spike that is used traditionally in ropework for teasing open strands or knots, but which was no doubt used in a variety of other situations. Most are fitted with a simple tin-opener blade with a lug that guided the blade around the edge of the tin while it was being used. While the average 'bully beef' tin did not require a special opener (being fitted with a key), other rations and tins supplied from home – such as condensed milk or Maconochie stew – needed the assistance of the opener. To prevent loss of the knife, it was worn with its large copper loop attached to a simple but sturdy string lanyard, tied invariably around the waist, the knife kept in the trouser pocket; in other cases, the lanyard would be passed over the left shoulder, the bulky knife held in the left breast pocket (the right pocket being the location of the soldier's paybook).

MESS TINS

In the first days of their service in the army men were issued with mess tins for eating their rations when in the line. Mess tins were intended to serve as both containers and cooking pots. Officially, the kit comprised the kidney-shaped two-part mess tin, with a shallow lid with fold-out handle, and a deeper tin with wire handle, contained in a canvas cover, though mounted troops were issued with a dish-like circular version. Both mess tins could be used for rudimentary cooking but as the tins were routinely inspected by an officer to see if they were clean this was not the preferred option for the 'old sweat', who would appropriate other utensils. In the line, tea was served in the deeper part of the tin; other cooked items, such as those brought up the line in large 'dixies' – holding 20 pints of food (divided between twenty men) from the company cooks – or in-trench cooked bacon, pork and beans or Maconochie's ration, would be eaten from the lid. The mess tin was originally to be carried in the haversack of the 1908-pattern equipment, but this made it unwieldy and difficult to access, as well as reducing stowage space. At the front line it was much more likely that soldiers wore their mess tins hung from the straps of the haversack, where they were accessible. Enamel mugs were also commonly carried in this way, as were the small canvas bags that contained the 'unexpired rations' from the day.

SHAVING KIT

For many young soldiers, shaving was a new experience, with downy cheeks requiring little more than a weekly shave. Army regulations required a clean chin, and, although the pre-war army had expected that soldiers would maintain a moustache, the upper lip was also kept cleanly shaven. The standard issue was a Sheffield-produced cut-throat razor – usually with horn fittings, but often of black plastic, upon which the soldier was expected to punch his regimental number and unit, in this case, the 1st Suffolk Regiment. Safety razors, a relatively new invention by the American K. C. Gillette, had been available from 1904, and soldiers unused to an open blade bought their own – together with a wide variety of shaving soaps, provided in tins. Shaving brushes, originally part of the soldiers' 'free kit' issue, soon ran out of bristles and were replaced from YMCA and Expeditionary Force canteens. Also useful were steel mirrors, unlikely to shatter and useful both for shaving and as impromptu signalling aids or periscopes; they were sold by Boots the Chemist 'for the man at the front'. Other men simply appropriated shaving mirrors, like this more fragile version carried by a private of the King's (Liverpool Regiment) – which nevertheless survived the war. Shaving in the dregs of cold tea from mess tins was common at the front, especially as warm water was a valuable commodity: its drawback was the soap scum that was difficult to remove from mugs, tainting further tea issues.

CLEANING KIT

Brushes were essential pieces of soldier's kit. Clothing Regulations from 1914 specified, in addition to shaving and tooth brushes, at least five other brushes issued as part of the soldier's 'necessaries': a hairbrush; a brush for cleaning the serge uniform; a polishing brush for brass; a brush for cleaning web equipment (applying the patent 'Blanco' cleaner made by the manufacturer Pickerings); a boot brush for applying dubbin; and another for providing a shine to the army boot while out of the front line. Clothes brushes typically had white and black bristles, boot brushes plain bristles, and equipment brushes a rectangular shape, to avoid confusion. All these brushes added to the weight to be carried by the front-line soldier – they would be consigned to storage with the large pack while Tommy was in the front line, to reappear when out on rest. One of the first chores for a new soldier was learning to keep his buttons bright, through the use of a button stick and a tin of 'Soldier's Friend'. The button stick was a simple plate of brass with a slot; it was placed behind the button during application of substances such as the 'Soldier's Friend', thus allowing the buttons to be polished without fear of staining the uniform. However, as the 1908 webbing also had a range of brass fitments, it was found that the normal button stick did not allow the webbing straps to be passed through easily, so by 1917 at least two patents were placed for more sophisticated 'equipment protectors'.

OFFICERS' KIT

Newly commissioned officers were expected to purchase their own uniforms and equipment. Readily assembled 'kit' was available from most of the West End stores. Harry Hall, 'The Recognised House for Officers' Service Dress & Equipment', in Oxford Street, London W1, offered complete kits 'for immediate wear or to order in 24 hours', while H. Graham Bennet, 'Uniform Specialist' of Moorgate, advertised their estimate for outfitting an infantry officer on joining: £34 2s 6d. The expense was considerable, especially as ill-advised subalterns could be tempted to buy kit that would prove superfluous in the trenches. Officers' kit was based around the Sam Browne belt – normally with a single cross-strap, but sometimes with double straps; this belt usually supported, in the early war period, the sword frog (soon discarded), the service revolver in a leather holster, an ammunition pouch, a canvas haversack, and a waterproof cotton map case and message pad. A leather-cased torch, with bull's-eye lens, was invariably worn on the belt. Separate from these, often carried by a fully laden officer using leather cross-straps, were a vernier compass in leather case, a water bottle and binoculars. A walking stick ('ash plant') was also *de rigueur*. Bedecked like Christmas trees, awkward new officers were often distinguished by the untried nature of their equipment, a fact remarked upon by Lieutenant Bernard Adams of the Welsh Regiment on his way to the front in 1915: 'Revolvers leapt from brand-new holsters; flash lamps and torches, compasses, map-cases, all were shown with an easy confidence of manner that screened a sinking dread of disapprobation.'

WEBLEY MARK VI

The large, heavy .455 calibre Webley Mark VI revolver was the standard side-arm of the British soldier during the Great War. Bought as the 'Service Revolver' by most officers, this distinctive weapon was also issued to machine-gunners and tank crews, men who required a revolver in case their principal weapons were rendered useless. The Mark VI was first introduced in May 1915 and became the most common service revolver used by the end of the war. It replaced the Mark IV, which had seen much service in the Boer War, and the Mark V, which was an updated and strengthened version that was introduced in 1913; both had 4-inch barrels and a 'bird's-head' butt, and fired .38 calibre bullets. The larger Mark VI was distinguished by its longer, 6-inch barrel, its square butt, and its larger, 'man-stopping' bullet; it was nevertheless difficult to aim effectively and had a maximum range of 50 yards – though, even then, hitting the target was a challenge. The weapon was holstered on the belt and was attached to a simple looped lanyard that was worn around the neck, intended to prevent the gun being dropped into the mud or dust often experienced while on active service. While officers' holsters were typically equipped with a flap, fastened with a brass post, those issued to other ranks were open-topped with a simple strap that was worn with webbing equipment and a small ammunition pouch. Some 300,000 Mark VI Webleys were made for war service.

TRENCH WHISTLE

The whistle has entered the mythology of the war, the image of the junior subaltern blowing a whistle at zero hour to signify the attack 'over the bags' being accepted as an icon. Most were made in Birmingham by the famous firm of Hudson's, the manufacturer of the 'Metropolitan' police whistle and its military versions since the mid-nineteenth century. Its distinctive shape was so designed that it could be held in the mouth while keeping the hands free, and at full blast its sound was found to carry for over a mile. Great War whistles are usually dated, stamped with the year of manufacture, and more than a million were made during the war years. Whistles were used not only to signal an impending attack, however; they were commonly employed on other tasks, warning of gas attacks for instance, or, more usually, by day sentries keeping watch through periscopes for incoming 'minies' – *minenwerfer* trench mortars. These were easily spotted in flight, and sentries would blow their whistles and shout 'minies to the left' or 'right', as appropriate. 'Acme' referees' whistles, snail-shaped and equipped with an internal pea, thereby imparting a completely different timbre, were also used – but by artillerymen, while giving orders in the preparation and laying of guns and howitzers. They too were dated. Both types would be worn attached to lanyards, or by simple leather tabs to a tunic button, or even incorporated in a convenient leather holder built into the cross-strap of the Sam Browne belt.

SMOKING

Cigarettes were brought up with the rations, and everyone was issued with a fair share. W. D. & H. O. Wills of Bristol produced many of the favoured brands – 'Gold Flake' and 'Woodbines' being common. Smoking was a means of killing time, of filling the void between meals and routine. It was also a means both of combating the stench of war and, in the Middle East at least, of deterring the plagues of flies. Tobacco and cigarettes were often supplied to front-line troops as a 'comfort', as part of Princess Mary's Christmas gift to the troops in December 1914, and in campaigns such as that run by the *Weekly Despatch* newspaper, which organised a 'tobacco fund'. Chain smoking was the norm in the line, a remedy for frayed nerves. With 'fags' so prevalent, obtaining a light from matches or lighters was essential. The supply of matches during the war was restricted – because timber was required for other purposes – and the supply of chemicals was difficult to maintain. This, together with the fact that matches are susceptible to dampness, meant that match folds and safes – including a special, tightly lidded 'Active Service' case produced by Bryant & May – became popular to protect what became a scarce resource. Lighters were also common, from the early-war 'tinder lighter' to 'trench art' lighters made from bullets and other waste materials. Requiring specialist equipment to construct, wartime examples were undoubtedly produced in ordnance and engineer workshops in the rear areas.

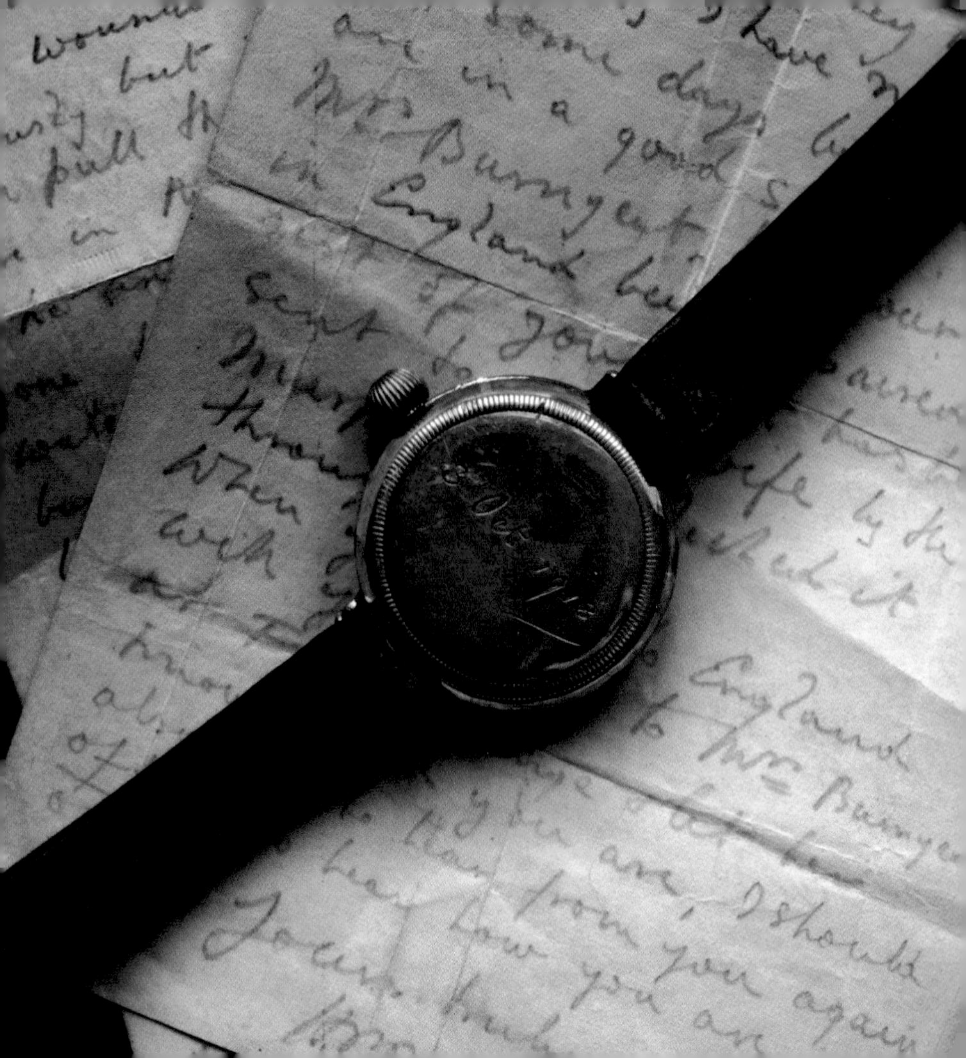

WRISTWATCH

Before the Great War, the wristwatch had been a fashionable accessory for ladies, but with the exigencies of wartime, and being less cumbersome than the pocket watch, it became re-branded as the 'trench watch', retailed by companies such as Mappin & Webb at a price of £2 10s. To equip them for active service, 'trench watches' typically had the number twelve picked out in red, or were equipped with luminous numerals, and guards were developed to protect watch crystals. The wearing of wristwatches by soldiers on active service was by no means confined to officers: this example (the reverse of which is shown) was worn by Driver Percy Boswell of the 65th Brigade, Royal Field Artillery. Driver Boswell, groom to Lieutenant Colonel Hugh Ponsonby Burnyeat RFA, was wounded in action by shellfire on 3 October 1918. Colonel Burnyeat was careful to write to Boswell's wife: 'I am very sorry to have to write and tell you that Boswell was wounded this morning. We were in the middle of heavy fighting … when a shell burst close. Boswell's is a deep wound across the back.' The colonel took time to write to his groom two weeks later: 'Mrs Burnyeat has your watch in England being repaired, the rest of your kit has been sent to your wife.' Mrs Burnyeat had the date of his wounding engraved on the back of it. While Boswell was invalided from the army and wore the watch for the rest of his life, his colonel was not so fortunate. He was killed by shellfire almost a month after his groom was wounded, and lies now in Bousies Communal Cemetery, near Le Cateau.

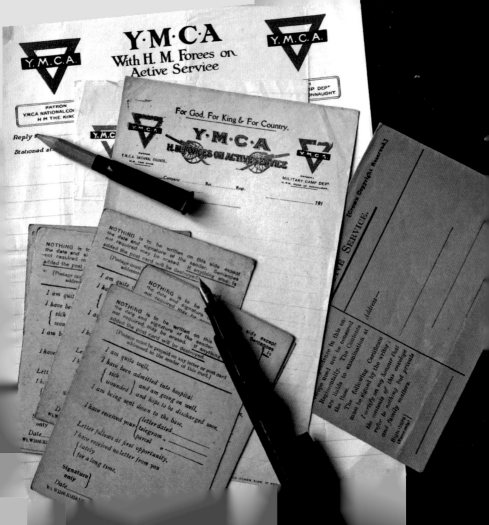

LETTERS

Letters to and from the front were of great importance in maintaining the morale of the troops. For the soldiers themselves, it was sufficient to write 'On Active Service' on the card or envelope, and the letter would be posted, carrying the postmark or cachet of the army field post-office. For most soldiers, the preferred means of writing their letters was the ubiquitous copy ink pencil. The fountain pen, although much promoted by companies such as Swan, was too impractical under service conditions, as specified in the *Field Service Regulations*. Each letter would be censored by an officer, who would append his signature to say that he had read its contents, but who would strike through passages that represented a security risk with a blue pencil. Green 'honour' envelopes were provided for deeply personal correspondence, however; soldiers had to sign a declaration stating they contained nothing sensitive in a military sense. The stationery used by soldiers was bought locally in shops in the base or rear areas, supplied from home, obtained from the many YMCA and Church Army huts, or gathered from 'comforts funds' set up at home. But often the humble field-service postcard was the means of getting a simple message home without having to go to the trouble of writing a long letter. Supplied by the military authorities, all that was required was that the sender cross out a few lines in order to get his message across, usually expressing the view that all was fine, and that 'letter follows at earliest opportunity'.

PHRASE BOOK

Transported to a foreign country, Tommy quickly picked up enough French to get by, just as he had in India as a pre-war regular. A variety of pidgin French was soon developed, despite the efforts of the authorities to encourage proficiency. 'Napoo' was a particular favourite, meaning 'no more', 'finished', 'broken', 'worn-out' or 'useless'; it was derived from '*Il n'y en a plus*' ('There is no more'). 'No compree' (derived from *compris*), which meant that there was no understanding on either side, was also common. For centuries, British soldiers serving abroad had appropriated words from the local language to fill in or supplement their own vocabulary. The languages of the Indian subcontinent provided many of the common examples, both in official parlance – khaki, puttee, and in soldier speak – 'Blighty' (for 'home'), 'bundook' (for 'rifle'). Adoption of pidgin French was therefore inevitable. Numerous French-language handbooks and pamphlets – even packet inserts like that provided with Black Cat cigarettes – were issued to tempt the soldiery away from their army slang, albeit with limited success. *The Soldiers' English-French Conversation Book (For the Man at the Front)* is typical, and includes phrases that, it was hoped, might make the job of the front-line soldier in France a little more intelligible. Military phrases included the hopeful '*Ils demandent un armistice*' ('They ask for an armistice'), rendered for the Tommy as 'Il der-mand un nar-mee-steess', through '*Baissez le tête*' ('Keep your head down!') or 'Bay-say lah tait' to the rather more urgent '*Sauve qui peut!*' ('Run for your life'), given, in case it was needed, as 'sov-kee-per'.

STEEL HELMET

Steel helmets were an innovation that was born out of the necessity of modern war. Until 1915 Tommy wore the Service Dress cap in all its forms in the front line. Head wounds were common as a consequence, especially with snipers intent on an easy shot and concentrating on movement past loopholes and dips in the trench sides. Clearly there was a need for increased head protection. The British steel helmet of 1915 was designed by John Leopold Brodie, who proposed a simple, easy-to-manufacture, dish-like helmet that could be punched from a single sheet of steel, with a liner that would reduce the effects of impact. The shape of the helmet was designed to resist spent bullets, as well as shrapnel falling from above – the wide rim deflecting low-energy impacts. Originally made from mild steel, it was soon manufactured from harder, non-magnetic manganese steel; its liner was composed initially of a crown pad of felt with lint layers, with a head band containing twelve tubular rubber spacers – all intended to lessen impact. After some trials, the helmet was adopted on 24 September 1915; over one million War Office Pattern helmets were supplied to the army in time for the Battle of the Somme in July 1916. Ironically, the incidence of head wounds appeared to rise – but only because a great number of men survived their injuries. The helmet was a success. Improvements were made to the helmet rim and liner in late 1916, producing the Mark 1 that is illustrated, the property of an officer of the 16th (Service) Battalion of the Nottinghamshire and Derbyshire Regiment.

SMLE RIFLE

The principal weapon of the British soldier from 1904 was the Short Magazine Lee Enfield rifle, the SMLE to most soldiers. The SMLE was based on its predecessor, the nineteenth-century Magazine Lee Enfield (MLE) rifle. The SMLE, however, was shorter, capable of being used by both infantry and cavalry. The charger system used by the SMLE allowed for five rounds to be loaded at a time, the magazine holding ten altogether. With its high-capacity magazine and efficient bolt action, in the right hands the rifle had an impressive rate of fire. Well-trained soldiers could fire around fifteen aimed bullets a minute with the SMLE, a rate unmatched by other armies. As the 'soldier's best friend', it was mandatory to keep the rifle clean, especially in the front line where it was needed the most. In and out of the trenches, breech and barrel were examined carefully for any sign of the dirt that would render a weapon unserviceable. To achieve this, all soldiers had to be proficient in arms drill, and competent in handling and cleaning their arms. A worn rifle would be inaccurate and a liability; with care, a rifle could be expected to fire at least five thousand rounds before it became unserviceable. The SMLE was provided with a cleaning kit consisting of a brass oil bottle containing machine oil ('Russian petroleum'), a brass-weighted cord 'pull-through' that was used to drag a piece of oiled flannelette cloth through the bore to clean it, or, when used with gauze, to scour residue left by firing the rifle. Regulations stipulated that this kit should be kept in the butt of the rifle, not separately within the haversack. Under trench conditions, however, keeping the rifle clean was a trying task.

1907-PATTERN BAYONET

With the development of a new, shorter rifle came the need for a longer bayonet, because the likely enemy of the British soldier would be equipped with the longer Mauser-type rifle, putting Tommy at a disadvantage in a lunging bayonet fight. The original bayonet issued with the SMLE, the 1903 pattern, was only 12 inches long, inadequate to counter the threat of German blades. As such, the 1907-pattern bayonet – always referred to as a 'sword' in British rifle regiments – was 5 inches longer than its predecessor; this would provide a reach comparable with any other existing weapons. The 1907-pattern bayonet attached to the SMLE by the use of a boss on the snub nose of the SMLE (beneath the muzzle), and a bayonet bar, connecting with the mortise groove on the pommel of the bayonet. Early versions had hooked quillons; by 1914 these had been superseded by the simpler version with an uncomplicated crosspiece. Both versions had simple leather scabbards with steel top-mounts and tips (chapes) that were carried suspended from the belt by simple frogs. Bayonet fighting drill was a significant component of the infantryman's training. Soldiers were required to understand the various stances that ensured correct poise and balance, and the means of parrying the rifle and bayonet in the hands of an enemy with deadly intent. For many soldiers, the sheer brutality of bayonet fighting was challenging; for High Command, inculcating the 'spirit of the bayonet' was at the heart of the army's 'offensive spirit'.

ENTRENCHING TOOL

Getting close to the earth was a natural reaction under fire; improving the cover of one's position required tools. All British infantrymen were equipped with a clever personal entrenching (officially 'intrenching') tool, which comprised a steel head of combined spade and pick, and a separate wooden handle called a helve. Carried in a holder of either webbing or leather (in the 1908- and 1914-pattern equipment sets, respectively), these tools were supplied to provide a means of digging a shallow scrape in an emergency, or for a multitude of other small jobs in the field, acting as hammer, pick and digging tool. It is doubtful that entrenching tools were used to dig many trenches, however; for that, the ubiquitous British GS shovel was needed. GS shovels were issued at the rate of 110 per battalion; open-mouthed, with a turned-back top to protect the heavily booted foot of the infantryman, these spades were used in earnest in the digging of front-line trenches. The time estimated in 1914 (as prescribed by the officers' *Field Service Pocket Book*) for digging a man's length-of-fire trench (two paces or 45 cubic feet) was a hundred minutes under normal conditions. Heavy picks were also provided where the ground was hard enough to warrant them, with seventy-six per battalion. Both tools would be used in digging trenches throughout the war. Under the orders of Engineer officers and NCOs, the infantry would provide the manpower to do so. Infantrymen were often to carry shovels (and picks) into action, such as by the leading assault troops on the Somme in 1916. This was to allow for the turning of trench lines once captured, with the reversal of the fire-step from one side to the other.

BARBED-WIRE CUTTERS

With the growing complexity of barbed wire came the increased necessity to cut it, to prevent being left 'hanging on the old barbed wire' in the aftermath of an attack, in the words of a popular soldier's song. One's own wire was almost as hazardous as that of the enemy, and special paths had to be cut through the tangled maze of wires, lanes that could be targeted by enterprising machine-gunners and snipers. To cut the enemy's wire was a hazardous job; wire would be attached to such warning signals as empty tin cans that would clatter alarmingly if approached. Early cutters were largely inadequate; a great variety was tried and patented, and many were tested by the Royal Engineers' experimental trench workshops. A variety of long-handled versions made from 1917 by Chater Lea was more satisfactory, but actually using the things was still fraught with difficulties. Wire-cutter attachments, to be fixed to the muzzle of an infantryman's SMLE, were also made. At least three versions were put into use during the war; this ungainly piece of equipment fed the wire on to jaws, which then pivoted when withdrawn to make a cut. Given the great tangles encountered, these cutters were never a practical proposition in the field. In many cases, cutting the wire was left to the artillery; a skilled business, it required shrapnel to burst at the correct height to obtain the desired effect. History shows that this was not always achieved.

TRENCH MAPS

With the development of trench warfare came the necessity of trench mapping. Good maps are of great value in any battle, supplying a wealth of information about topographical position for vantage, and the nature of the 'going', the surfaces over which man and materiel would need to travel. When the Allies went to war they relied upon their state surveys, and those of their friends, to provide military maps that might aid in the deployment of troops and the ranging of artillery. While those for the Western Front – France and Belgium – were of good quality generally, information available on fronts in the Middle East was in some cases less reliable. In 1915, with the move to static warfare on most fronts, trenches started to be overprinted on existing maps, with the best examples being in France and Flanders. Here, at scales of 1:20,000 and 1:10,000, special trench maps were produced that plotted the location of trenches, and used a semi-formal nomenclature for ruined structures and trenches that grew up in the front line, and which was perpetuated by the Survey Companies of the Royal Engineers. The convention for trench maps from 1915 to 1917 was to show the German trenches in red, the British – in outline only – in blue; in 1918, this convention was reversed. Regular updates were created in advance of trench raids and offensives, and secret editions created. Not surprisingly, millions of trench maps were produced during the war, at all scales. From these humble documents, great offensives such as the Somme, Passchendaele and the Advance to Victory in 1918 were planned and prosecuted; in developing these maps, many men of the Royal Flying Corps, flying stable camera platforms vulnerable to enemy 'scouts', lost their lives taking aerial photographs.

SBR (GAS MASK)

The use of gas on 22 April 1915 by the Germans during their assault at Ypres took the Allies unawares, and between eight hundred and fourteen hundred men were killed and a further two to three thousand men injured by the gas. Primitive respirators were pressed into service containing field dressings soaked in bicarbonate of soda – or even urine – to combat the suspected chlorine, and this evolved into a pad of cotton waste soaked with sodium hyposulphite and other chemicals. Clearly inadequate, these pads were replaced by a hood that covered the whole head, its tail being tucked into the tunic to provide a seal. At first the hood had a simple mica window, but the later helmets possessed eyepieces and an outlet valve. All were soaked in sodium phenate, and later hexamine – highly absorbent of phosgene gas – to become the Phenate-Hexamine or PH Helmet. All were clammy, cloying and unpleasant to wear. The PH Helmet could stop only a limited amount of gas, however, and in 1916 it was replaced with a mask that used a 'box' of stacked granules of lime-permanganate, pumice soaked in sodium sulphate, and charcoal. The Small Box Respirator (SBR) issued in August 1916 had a box with lime-permanganate granules between two layers of charcoal. It was fitted with an exhalation valve and carried in a haversack that could be hitched up on to the chest (strap over the head) into the 'alert' position. When wearing it, the soldier gripped its inner rubber mouthpiece between his teeth, and used the integrated nose clip to ensure his breathing was through the 'box'. This mask was to prove highly effective.

MILLS BOMB

The British Army went to war with little regard for hand grenades. They possessed only one type – the No. 1, which had a long handle with streamers to facilitate a good throw, especially with its cast-iron weighted head containing the explosive charge. But it was complex to arm, and was fitted with a percussion fuse that made it vulnerable when in the confines of a trench. The War Office was forced to try out other, inadequate designs for the battles of 1915. The mass-produced No. 15 resembled a cricket ball. It could be thrown a reasonable distance, but it relied on a friction fuse that was badly affected in wet weather – not ideal in Flanders. Not surprisingly, it was replaced by the Mills Bomb, officially designated the No. 5 grenade. The secret of its success lay with its ignition system, which used a striker that was activated when a pin was removed and a lever released; the lever was then ejected and a four-second fuse activated, during which time the bomber had to throw the grenade. The body of the grenade was formed of cast iron, and weighed 1 pound 6½ ounces; its surface was divided into sections to promote fragmentation. Coloured bands indicated its fillings: pink for ammonal, green for amatol. The grenade had a centrepiece that contained separate cavities for the striker and the detonator. The striker was kept cocked against a spring, the striker lever holding the striker firmly in position when held against the body of the bomb, locked there by the action of the split safety pin until the bomber removed the pin and threw the grenade. When the bomb was thrown, the lever flew off, thereby releasing the striker.

GRENADE BADGES

Among the most significant weapons of the trench war were the grenade and the trench mortar. Infantry assault on trenches changed as the war progressed; in the early stages of the war, infantry would attack with rifle and fixed bayonet, and the grenade was very much an ancillary weapon – and the British Army was inadequately supplied with these at the outbreak of war. This changed with the introduction of the Mills Bomb in 1915. From then onwards, 'bombing down' a trench meant working from traverse to traverse, with men to lead, men to carry and others left to 'mop up'. From 1915 trained 'bombers' were awarded a red flaming grenade to wear on their sleeves (officers' versions were distinguished by a white ball). If grenades supplanted rifles, then trench mortars represented mobile trench artillery. The first effective British trench mortars – high-trajectory, low-range but high-explosive weapons capable of dealing a blow to any trench and its occupants – included the 'toffee apple', introduced in mid-1915. Officially the 2-inch Medium Trench Mortar, it lobbed a 42-pound spherical bomb from a 2-inch diameter tube; a single round could destroy 6 square yards of barbed wire. More reliable was the Stokes Mortar, a simple 3-inch drainpipe affair: Stokes bombs were dropped into the tube, a striker activating the charge and propelling the round up to 1,500 yards. As with bombers, from 1916 the sleeves of trench mortar men were distinguished by flaming grenades – but worked in blue. Both bombers and mortar men were unpopular with the infantry – as more often than not they were the target of enemy retaliation. For this reason, both groups were believed to belong to the 'suicide club'.

TRENCH KNIVES

In most cases, the British 1907-pattern bayonet was too long to be effective in trench raids. As no official knives were issued to British troops, home-made examples were actively employed. According to expert Anthony Saunders, the knife was not a preferred weapon on British trench raids; trench clubs were more commonly used. While the Americans, the Germans and even the French were issued with short knives for battle use, the British often resorted to privately purchased examples from such stores as the Army and Navy in London, or to manufacturing their own close to the front line. Typical of this industry was the use of cut-down bayonets, like this 1907-pattern Lee Enfield bayonet (far right), cut down and shaped to a more manageable blade, or the more ancient 1876 French Gras bayonet (right), again commonly reduced. Also popular was the Canadian Ross bayonet, which was issued for the ill-fated Ross rifle, a weapon that was withdrawn as being unfit for front-line service in late 1916 (far left). Already relatively short, it was a handy weapon, and the muzzle ring was removed to make it even handier. The 'French nail' was a piece of bent steel fashioned into a crude handle with a sharp tip, but any suitable piece of metal that would carry a blade was also pressed into service. Saunders records the use of ground-down metal files; the example illustrated (left), based on a file made in Sheffield, is typical of this type. Together with trench clubs, these crudely fashioned knives are gruesome reminders of a terrible war.

RUM JAR

The issue of a rum ration in the armed forces was a British institution. Service rum was thick and fiery; its positive effects after a night on the fire-step are remembered in most soldiers' memoirs. Rum was issued from ceramic jars labelled or impressed 'SRD'. These initials stood for 'Supply Reserve Depot', which was a large army supply establishment based in Deptford on the site of a Tudor royal dockyard and later cattle market. The depot was leased from the Corporation of London to the many rum warehouses on the river front that supplied the contents of the jars. The jars themselves were made by several potteries, with Doulton of Lambeth and Pearson & Co of Staffordshire being amongst the most prolific. In the trenches, rum was issued at dawn and dusk, following 'Stand to'; its fiery warmth intended to help cheer men plagued with cold, wet or otherwise miserable conditions. It was also issued to those men about to go 'over the bags', either at dawn with a large-scale attack, or at night prior to a raid. The rum ration was issued by a senior NCO, with an officer in attendance. Because drunkenness was a serious offence, the ration could not be accumulated and saved for later; it was poured into a mug or mess-tin top and had to be drunk in the presence of the officer. It was a long-held belief that any rum residue left in a jug was taken by the sergeant – a perk of his position. Soldiers were otherwise not entitled to alcohol in the trenches.

MARCH, 1917.

Monday 26

MARCH—APRIL, 1917.

Friday 30

Tuesday 27

MARCH

7 Sun—3rd in

8 Mo

9 Tues

10 Wed

Mem

COLLINS'
COMPACT DIARY
FOR
1916.

CONTAINING COUPON FOR
£1000 ACCIDENT INSURANCE,
GIVING GREATEST BENEFITS.
Covering also Weekly Payments in case of
Disablement, and many other advantages.

To order this Diary give Number
stamped on cover.
For complete list of other bindings
see Order Form inside.

LONDON AND GLASGOW:
COLLINS'
CLEAR-TYPE PRESS.

RCH

DIARIES

The keeping of personal diaries was frowned upon officially. With the war in stalemate and largely static, the chance of diaries falling into the hands of the enemy was high, especially as trench raiding parties were sent over by both sides to try to capture prisoners, or to gather intelligence through the collection of insignia or by picking up paperwork, letters and orders. Despite this, diary manufacturer Charles Letts produced a range of pocket editions that could easily be carried in the jacket pocket, and even marketed 'The Soldier's Own Diary' for the war years from 1915 to 1919. It was packed with information such as the semaphore alphabet, the main ranks of the army and European decorations, and each page also carried useful tips and simple facts, such as how to make bridges, and what the penetrating power of bullets was. The diaries illustrated were the property of Private Humphrey Mason, a Kitchener volunteer with the 6th Battalion Oxfordshire & Buckinghamshire Light Infantry who went on to serve as a sergeant with the Machine Gun Corps. Battered, they were carried in Mason's pocket and were no doubt sent home. On this matter, the *Field Service Regulations* were firm:

In no circumstances is specific reference to be made … in private diaries sent from the theatre of operations, to the place from which they are written or despatched; to the plans of future operations whether rumoured, surmised or known; to the armament of troops or fortresses; to defensive works; to the moral and physical condition of the troops; to casualties previous to the publication of official lists… Criticism of operations is forbidden.

LORD ROBERTS'
MESSAGE.

25th Aug. 1914

I ask you to put your
trust in God. He will watch
over you and strengthen you.
You will find in this little
Book guidance when you are
in health, comfort when you are
in sickness, and strength when
you are in adversity.

Rober[...]

Pte J. Brock.
Royal West Surrey's
"The Queens"
N.º 1764
A Coy.

PRESENTED BY C.O.
SEPT. 6ᵀᴴ 14

TESTAMENT

Small Bibles, or 'Active Service Testaments', were commonly carried by soldiers in the field. Measuring just 3½ inches by 2½ inches, these books were designed to be carried in a pocket or haversack, and were intended to provide comfort to soldiers suffering under fire. On more than one occasion, these small books helped to save the lives of their owners in a physical sense – stopping the passage of a bullet in flight. Produced by the Scripture Gift Mission, the Naval and Military Bible Society and other charitable Christian organisations such as the YMCA, these copies of the New Testament were given out to those who requested them, or, as in this case, were given as gifts by commanding officers or family members in the hope that they would provide comfort to the men going to war. The majority carried the words of Field Marshal Lord Roberts, commonly known as 'Bobs', written on 25 August 1914: 'I ask you to put your trust in God. He will watch over you and strengthen you. You will find in this little Book guidance when you are in health, comfort when you are in sickness, and strength when you are in adversity. Roberts, FM.' A hero of the British army in the late nineteenth century, Lord Roberts was widely respected, particularly by the Army of India. He died of pneumonia in Belgium in November 1914, while 'doing his duty' visiting Indian troops.

Army Form...

No. 10. Regiment R.E. (Postal Section...

PASS. Permanent.

No. 182664 (Rank) Spr (Name) Jack...

has permission to be absent from his quarters, from

1st February. to 28th Feb...

for the purpose of proceeding to Etaples & Pa...

(Station) Etaples.

(Date...

H.M. FORCES OVERSEAS (IN UN...

Combined Leave and Railway...

Available for an authorised journey on the Ra...
Britain and Ireland (including the Underground...
on the Steamers running to and from the Ports...

No. H 369323

Third C...

FOR ONE PERS...

From Edinburgh...

(Any alteration will render the Ticket...
unless made and signed by a Railway...
Transport Officer.)

To FRANCE.

Leave granted from 28.10.18 to 11.11.18

This Ticket is to be shown on Demand, but is to be retained
by the Holder until the rejoins his Unit when it is to be given
up to the issuing Officer.

Through tickets in cases where the journey is not continuous do not
include the cost of transfer between Railway Termini in Towns or between
Railway Stations and Steamboats.

This Ticket is issued subject to the Regulations of the respective
Companies over whose Lines it is available, and to the Conditions stated
in their Time Tables.

No....

DINNER.

On presentation of this ticket
at the E.F.C. HAVRE, the
bearer is entitled to

DINNER

free of charge.

2,000,000. 1/19. P.P.Ltd. E. 4409.

No....

TEA.

On presentation of this ticket
at the E.F.C., HAVRE, the
bearer is entitled to

TEA

free of charge.

LEAVE PASS

On average, and if they were lucky, soldiers returned home on leave once a year. Officers fared better, with a leave granted at around four months, but it was still a rare commodity. Detailed direct from the front line, men would have to find their way back on the laborious trail home – and if they lived in a more remote part of the British Isles, this could be a long trek indeed. Issued with a pass to get through the lines – with Military Police on the look-out for 'stragglers' and those with intent to desert military service (with dire consequences) – the soldier would usually start his journey on foot, but, if he was fortunate, he might pick up a lift from passing Army Service Corps (ASC) motor transport on the way to a railhead. From here, and using his warrant to travel, he would get to one of the main ports for cross-Channel leave traffic, most often Le Havre. At Le Havre food might be obtained from the Expeditionary Force Canteens (EFC), before he boarded a steamer bound for Folkestone, from where he would take a train to London. Travel onwards would take men to their home destination, sometimes at quite a distance. Those men in France and Flanders were at least able to get to 'Blighty' in relatively short order; home leave from more remote fronts was more difficult. When they got home men would distribute souvenirs gained at the front – but more often than not they would avoid all other talk of conditions, as they tried to forget the mud of the trenches.

TRENCH ART

Collecting souvenirs of service was common amongst soldiers; more often than not these included artillery nose caps and small uniform items taken from prisoners and kept in packs until they were granted leave – an uncommon occurrence for most soldiers. In other cases, objects were fashioned into 'trench art', a kind of folk art using bullets, shell cases, copper drive bands, fragments of aircraft, pieces of wood and other detritus of war to manufacture souvenirs. With the vast array of materials available to the soldier of the Great War, trench art became ubiquitous. Some pieces were made by the British soldier in the front line, but most were fashioned by men in the rear areas, where there was more access to tools and equipment, or by prisoners of war. Typical soldier items include decorated shell cases, letter-openers, matchbox folds, lighters, tanks and field caps. Illustrated are match folds and a fuel bottle for a trench lighter that incorporate pieces of captured German belt buckle, with their distinctive motto *Gott mit uns* ('God with us') and the Prussian crown. Many pieces were actually made by enterprising civilians and garrison (and ancillary) troops in the battle zone, both during and after the war, but especially when a lucrative tourist market was developing post-war. Examples included tanks made from a variety of materials, field caps made from shell cases, letter openers, and matchbox covers. Companies at home also cashed in, mounting war souvenirs such as fuse caps as desk sets, dinner gongs or photograph frames.

SILK POSTCARDS

By far the most important souvenirs of front-line service collected by the British soldier in France and Flanders were silk postcards, which became a real phenomenon of the war. Though they had been first produced in 1907, the influx of soldiers provided a new market and the cards gained popularity early in 1915, when the locals realised the potential for marketing the results of their labours. Some estimates suggest that as many as ten million cards were produced during the war. Each card was produced as part of a cottage industry in which mostly women embroidered intricate designs by hand on to strips of silk mesh, the design being repeated as many as twenty-five times on a strip, before being sent to a factory for cutting and mounting as postcards and greetings cards. The cards themselves were bought from civilians trying to scrape a living from supplying the soldiers' needs in the immediate battle zone. They were not cheap, each one costing as much as three times the daily pay of the average soldier. Though true postcards, they were sold and sent home in simple envelopes intended to protect their precious contents. There is a huge range: sentimental messages – 'Friendship', 'Birthday Greetings', 'Home Sweet Home' and so on were popular and are very common – as are cards celebrating festivals and holidays. Many had delicately opening pockets with a small card insert; others would carry 'Greetings from France' or poignant messages 'From the Trenches'. But, for many soldiers, cards with intricately worked regimental crests were the most sought-after.

FIELD DRESSING

Field dressings were issued to all soldiers, to be kept in a pocket under the front flap of the Service Dress tunic. The First Field Dressing was intended for rudimentary first aid and consisted of a packet containing two dressings – one for the entry wound, one for the exit (in the case of gunshot wounds). Early on, these pouches also contained safety pins, and ampoules of iodine as a form of disinfectant to treat the wound; later in the war, after the value of the chemical had been questioned, it was left out of the set. In all cases, the idea was that a wounded man would have his wounds dressed with his own dressing. With so many wounds being caused by shellfire, larger dressings were needed than could be carried by an individual, and these special 'shell dressings' were carried in action by regimental stretcher-bearers. According to the official *Field Service Regulations*,

> The First Field Dressing applied as a protection against dirt and to stop haemorrhage, with the addition of some support to a broken limb, before removal of the patient, is all that is needed on the field itself. After this first aid, a wounded man should be left where he lies, under as good cover as possible, unless the nature of the ground, a pause in the fighting, or the approach of darkness allows systematic collection and removal.

STRETCHER-BEARER ARMBAND

Stretcher-bearers were battalion men who gave up their arms to carry their stretchers, the bearing of arms by medics being expressly forbidden in war. Ideally, at least six men would be needed per stretcher; this was not always achievable in the front line, and German prisoners were often drafted in to carry wounded soldiers back, as it was an offence under Field Service Regulations to escort wounded men back without the express permission of an officer. Regimental stretcher-bearers wore a brassard or armband bearing the initials 'SB'. Many were bandsmen; others were riflemen from each battalion who were detailed or volunteered for the job – a dangerous task, requiring service under fire, usually in no man's land. Being battalion men, stretcher-bearers would recognise their wounded comrades, who would call out for them in trenches and from shell holes. Unarmed, and sent out in often very trying conditions after battles and trench raids, it is not surprising that bearers would be cited for gallantry – in some cases winning the Victoria Cross for their actions, the highest award that could be bestowed. Regimental stretcher-bearers' responsibilities ended at the regimental aid post, however; from there men were dispatched to the rear areas, to be cared for under the auspices of the Royal Army Medical Corps. RAMC men wore the red Geneva cross; it was their role (as part of the wider jurisdiction of the Army Medical Services) to care for the wounded and evacuate them efficiently from the front line to, as was hoped by most soldiers, 'Blighty'.

CHELTENHAM
10. 45 AM
APR 20 16
CHELTENHAM
10. 45 AM
APR 20 16
ONE PENNY
78
2nd Lieut – H. W. Corke
1/1 T. M. B.,
1st Brigade.
British Expeditionary Force
R.E. (S.R)
F.P. ARN C.B.
Killed in Action
Certified by:-
Major
Staff Captain, 1st Infantry Brigade.

CASUALTY LETTER

Receiving a notification from the War Office was dreaded by all at home during the war; more often than not it would signify that a loved one had been killed, wounded or taken prisoner. For officers, this notification would come in the form of a telegram; for other ranks, it would be a proforma with spaces for the soldier's name, regiment and other details. But, because of delays in official notification, the first inkling of a casualty in some households might be a letter returned home with the brutal and stark message 'Killed in action' written or stamped on its unopened cover. This was the case for Second Lieutenant H. W. Corke of the 10th Battalion Gloucestershire Regiment, serving with trench mortars in France with the 1st Brigade, 1st Division. Having a notoriously risky occupation, trench mortar men were often targeted by their opponents. Lieutenant Corke landed in France in October 1916, and by 19 April 1917 he had been killed in action while in charge of a trench mortar battery. His parents learned the sad news when their letters to him were returned. He is buried in Maroc British Cemetery, Grenay. Fortunately, in many other cases, letters would be written by the adjutant or chaplain to soften the blow. These letters would usually profess that the soldier in question had died instantly and had not suffered, though the actual truth might be harder to bear.

WOUNDED STRIPES

Soldiers who had been wounded were permitted to wear a simple, vertically arranged 2-inch-long strip of gold 'Russian braid' on the left forearm of their uniform tunic; this distinguished the experienced soldier from the raw recruit. Wounded stripes were an innovation of 1916 and followed a suggestion made by Sir Arthur Conan Doyle that wounding should be recognised by some distinction. To receive the stripe, each soldier needed to have been listed in the casualty returns as 'wounded'. (The French followed suit in 1916 with the award of a multi-coloured ribbon with a silver star that was to be worn on the left breast of the uniform.) Simple in construction, one stripe was worn for each instance of wounding, though not for each wound received. In many cases, the 'Russian braid' material originally specified was not hard-wearing, and it was replaced by brass versions with backing strips, which could easily be removed for cleaning. Though it was the fervent hope of many soldiers that their wounds would see them home to 'Blighty' and thence out of the war, all too often, after a brief period of convalescence, they would be returned to the front – not necessarily their original battalion – and it is not unusual for contemporary photographs to show soldiers with multiple wounded stripes.

The War of 1914-1918.

Oxf. & Bucks. Light Infantry

No. 15511 Serjt. H. Mason, 6th Bn.

... mentioned in a Despatch from
... Sir Douglas Haig. K.T. G.C.B. G.C.V.O. K.C.I.E.
... dated 7th November 1917

... distinguished services in the Field.

... from the King to record His Majesty's

... of the services rendered.

Winston S. Churchill

Secretary of State for War.

MEDALS

Each soldier who served overseas received at least two medals for his service: the silver War Medal and the Victory Medal ('Mutt and Jeff'). If serving overseas in 1914 or 1915, the combination is the 1914–15 Star, the War Medal and the Victory Medal ('Pip, Squeak and Wilfred'). The 1914–15 Star was widely distributed, with some 2,350,000 awarded to the men who had seen action at the Second Battle of Ypres and in Gallipoli. For those men who had served in France before 22 November 1914, members of the original British Expeditionary Force, the 1914 Star took its place. The British War Medal ('Squeak'), minted in silver, depicts a man on horseback trampling a shield bearing the Imperial German eagle – symbolising man controlling a force of great strength. A skull and cross bones represent the casualties of the war, and the rising sun stands for peace; some 6.5 million of these medals were issued. Finally, the Victory Medal was typical of the many issued to the Allied nations, bearing the same ribbon – limiting the need to issue the British medal to other nationalities, for example. The British medal bears an Art Nouveau-inspired female figure of Victory, with the inscription 'The Great War for Civilisation' on the reverse; a total of 5,725,000 Victory Medals was awarded. Those who had been Mentioned in Dispatches (MID) were given a certificate and were granted the right to wear a bronze oak leaf on the ribbon of the Victory Medal. This trio, marked by the oak leaves, was awarded to Sergeant Humphrey Mason of the Machine Gun Corps – an original Kitchener volunteer who had survived the war.

POPPY

In 1921 the British Legion, combining four of the main old soldiers' organisations, was formed with Field Marshal Earl Haig as its first President. A special employment committee was set up, and employers were encouraged to take on at least five per cent war-disabled men. By 1925 the British Legion had formed 2,500 branches and had 145,000 members. Like many of the ex-servicemen's organisations, the Legion instigated travel groups to gravesides and battlefronts for relatives and old soldiers, notably the mass pilgrimage in 1928. The British Legion was to become associated with the poppy: one of the Legion's main devices for fund raising, artificial poppies and poppy emblems were sold to raise money for its charitable work. The emblem had first been used by an American, Moina Michael, who, inspired by John McCrae's poem 'In Flanders Fields', conceived the idea of wearing an artificial poppy in 1918 as a tribute to United States war veterans and to raise funds for disabled ex-servicemen. On 11 November 1921 the first British Poppy Day was held on the third anniversary of the end of the Great War; the appeal, known as the Haig Fund, raised £106,000. In 1922 Major George Howson formed the Disabled Society to aid disabled servicemen. At Howson's suggestion, a poppy factory was founded in Richmond in 1922. The poppy was designed so that disabled workers could easily assemble it, although complex wreaths and arrangements were available from catalogues – much in demand on Armistice Day.

INDEX

'Active Service Testaments' 99

Allenby, General 9

Argyll & Sutherland
  Highlanders 37

Arisaka rifle 25

Armistice 7, 73

Army Service Corps (ASC)
  5, 11, 12, 14, 15, 101

Barbed-wire cutters 83

Bayonet 79, 91, 93

Birmingham Pals 41

Black Watch 37

Blighty 23, 73, 101, 113

Boots 47

British Expeditionary Force
  (BEF) 4, 115

British Legion 117

Brodie, John Leopold 75

Bully beef 53

Button stick 49, 53

Cameron Highlanders 37

Cameronians 37

Cap badge 27, 33, 35, 37, 41

Cap, Service Dress 35, 41

Casualties 7, 15, 109, 111

Casualty letter 111

Church Army 71

Clasp ('Jack') knife 51, 53

Cleaning kit 59, 77

Diaries 97

Divisions 5, 31, 43, 111

Doyle, Sir Arthur Conan 113

Duke of Cornwall's Light
  Infantry 15

Egypt 11, 39

Entrenching tool 11, 81

Equipment, 1908 pattern
  (webbing) 11–13, 14, 15,
  55, 59, 81

Equipment, 1914 pattern
  (leather) 7, 12, 81

Expeditionary Force Canteen
  (EFC) 57, 101

Field dressings 107

Field Service Regulations 45, 71,
  97, 107

Formation sign 43

Gallipoli 7, 11, 39, 115

Gas mask 87

Glengarry 9, 37

Good-luck charms 19

Gordon Highlanders 9

Green envelopes 71

Grenade 89

Grenade badges 91

Haig, Field Marshal Earl 117

Haig Fund 117

Highland Light Infantry 37

Holdall 49

Identity discs 19, 45

Khaki Drill (KD) 11, 39

King's (Liverpool) Regiment
  37, 57

King's Own Scottish Borderers
  25, 37, 51

King's Royal Rifle Corps
  (KRRC) 15

Kitchener, Field Marshal Lord 4

Kitchener's Army 4, 12, 27, 31,
  37, 41, 43, 115

Leave 101, 103

Letters 71, 103, 111

Liverpool Scottish 37

Lloyd George, David 43

London Irish Rifles 31

Loos, Battle of 31, 51

Machine gun 51

Machine Gun Corps
  45, 97, 115

Maconochie ration 53, 55

McCrae, John 117

Matches 67, 103
Medals 21, 109, 115
Menin Gate 15
Mentioned in Despatches
    (MiD) 115
Mesopotamia 9, 11, 39
Mess tins 55
Middlesex Regiment 13, 31
Military Service Act 1916 5
Mills Bomb 89, 91
Mons, Battle of 7
'Mutt & Jeff' 115
'Napoo' 73
'Necessaries' 49, 59
Nottingham & Derbyshire
    Regiment 75
Officer's kit 61
Oxfordshire & Buckinghamshire
    Light Infantry 27, 97
Pals Battalion 41
Passchendaele (3rd Battle
    of Ypres) 85
Paybook 33, 53
PH helmet 87
Phrase book 73
'Pip, Squeak & Wilfred' 115
Poppy 117, 118
Postcards 71, 105
Puttees 10, 11, 73
Queen's (Royal West Kent
    Regiment) 9

Rations 51, 53
Roberts, Field Marshal Lord 99
Royal Army Medical Corps
    (RAMC) 5, 109
Royal Engineers 5, 81, 83, 85
Royal Field Artillery (RFA)
    5, 12, 69
Royal Flying Corps 85
Royal Fusiliers 31
Royal Naval Division (RND) 5
Royal Scots 37
Royal Scots Fusiliers 37
Royal Sussex Regiment 35
Rum jar 95
Salisbury Plain 27
Salonika 9, 39
Sam Browne belt 61
Scoring booklet (musketry) 25
Semaphore cards 29
Service Dress 10–11, 39,
    43, 107
Shaving kit 49, 57
Short, Magazine, Lee Enfield
    (SMLE) 7, 13, 25, 77, 79, 83
Signalling 29
Silks 105
Small Box Respirator (SBR) 87
Smoking 67
Somme, Battle of 5, 81, 85
Souvenirs 103, 105
Spoon 49

Sports medals 31
Steel helmet 75
Stretcher bearer 109
'Suicide Club' 91
Supply Reserve Depot (SRD) 95
Sweetheart jewellery 21
Tam O'Shanter 37
Territorials 4, 27, 37, 41
'Toffee apple' (2-inch Mortar) 91
'Tommy Atkins' 4, 47, 59
Training 23, 25, 27, 79
Trench art 21, 67, 103
Trench cap 35
Trench clubs 93
Trenches 85, 91
Trench knives 93
Trench maps 85
Trench mortar 65, 91, 111
Trench whistle 65
Tyneside Scottish 37
Webley Mark VI 63
Welsh Regiment 61
Western Front 7, 45, 47, 85
West Yorkshire Regiment 7
Wolseley Pattern helmet 11, 39
Worcestershire Regiment 21
Wounded stripes 113
Wristwatch ('trench watch') 69
YMCA 57, 71, 99
Ypres (Salient, Battles of)
    15, 85, 87, 115